Under Stars

For Ciarān, for *moja*

UNDER STARS

poems by —————————

TESS GALLAGHER

GRAYWOLF · 1978

Acknowledgement is made to the following periodicals in which som
of these poems first appeared: *Porch*, *Ontario Review*, *Back Door*, *Da*
Horse, *Borrowed Times*, *American Poetry Review*, *Ironwood*, *Quarter*
West, and *New York Review*. 'Under Stars' and 'Start Again Som
where' were first published by *The New Yorker*. 'Counterfeit Kisse
and 'The Same Kiss After Many Years' were printed in *Portable Kiss*
(Sea Pen Press, 1978).

Funding for this publication was provided in part by a grant from t
National Endowment for the Arts.

First edition

LC number 77-95331
ISBN 0-915308-19-3 (cloth)
      0-915308-20-7 (paper)

The Graywolf Press, PO Box 142, Port Townsend, Washington 983

Contents

The Ireland Poems

Start Again Somewhere

What is poetry? The mind of a child? Imagine two people in a room, a child and its father, and a horse going past in the street outside. The father looks out and says: 'There is Mary's horse going past.' That is a telling. From all appearances the father has lost the horse because he remains outside it. Say a horse is a disease. The father does not catch the disease. The horse does not enrich the father's life. But as for the child—he apprehends the sound of the horse. He tastes the sound of the horse for the sake of the sound itself. And he listens to the sound getting weaker and weaker and falling back into silence. And he wonders at the sound and he wonders at the silence. And he apprehends the rear legs of the horse and wonders at their authority and antiquity. And the world is filled with horsiness and the magic of reins. That is to be under another appearance. And that, I think, is poetry.

—Sean O'Riordán
(tr. by Ciarán Carson)

THE IRELAND POEMS

'Travelling is a brutality. It forces you to trust
strangers and to lose sight of all that familiar
comfort of home and friends. You are constantly
off balance. Nothing is yours except the essential
things—air, sleep, dreams, the sea, the sky—all
things tending toward the eternal or what we
imagine of it.'

—Pavese

Words Written Near a Candle

If I could begin anything
I'd say stop asking forgiveness, especially
theirs which was always
the fault mentioned in your condition.

Nettles could be feathers
the moment they brush your
ankle. At the same time: floods, earthquakes,
the various slaveries
hunchbacked near the fence
to catch your glance.

What is it to say that among the hired boats
we carried our bodies well, cracked
jokes, left the gaps
in our lives and not
the page? This far to learn
the boat does not touch the water!

And if this is goodbye,
it is a light nowhere near believing
and I am happy
and it is all right to make a distance
of a nearness, to say, 'Boat, I have left you
behind. Boat,
I am with you.'

Sligo Footraces

for Jo Jo

Between your arms hung on the fence,
the starter rushes along the line
instructing the forward foot,
the care an executioner
takes to see the tied hands are bound.

He runs his eye along the ground
and in his black coat, the raised gun fired
the instant the others break
from you in your race, leaving
a clean, invisible pit in your skull,
a lateness we can't make up—
as though your colt of a body
among the twelve-year-olds were ours
out of time, in time to tell us
we happen awake
in moments not our own.

I would wake again
to see you run
in the pack and late
though the instant I write this
I am gone
and you a man behind me, late
over the soft ground
of the children.

Four Dancers at an Irish Wedding

It was too simple and too right,
the father blue-eyed
and doting, his daughter a mock-up
of the bride in her long dress, earrings
and matching steps.

Red shirt, I am right
for you, wrong for you. Here
is my cheek forever
in this careless waltz
where we chanced to meet.

Darling, darling, darling

in the sob-throated beat
and we are true, my sad-eyed partner,
truest to complicate the step, taking
this father's hand, this child's.

The circle opens and closes
where our joined hands meet. Sweet
gladness, I
am not yours
and you are not mine. Break. Break
where the beat widens, take
the worried girl, leave me
the father.

Darling, darling, darling

we are all stolen and grieving
in the tender arms.
I have seen the magpie in the morning
on the back of a cow
singing: One
is for sorrow. One
is for sorrow.

Drop the strange hand, be
lifted, child, held
there on your father's swaying shoulder
for we are one and one and
one with ourselves
on the polished floor.

Women's Tug of War at Lough Arrow

In a borrowed field they dig in their feet
and clasp the rope. Balanced
against neighboring women, they hold
the ground by the little gained
and leaning like boatmen rowing into
the damp earth, they pull
to themselves the invisible waves, waters
overcalmed by desertion
or the narrow look trained to a brow.

The steady rain has made girls of them,
their hair in ringlets. Now they haul
the live weight to the cries
of husbands and children, until the rope
runs slack, runs free
and all are bound again by the arms
of those who held them, not until, but so
they gave.

Love Poem to Be Read to an Illiterate Friend

I have had to write this down
in my absence and yours. These
things happen. Thinking
of a voice added
I imagine a sympathy outside us
that protects the message
from what can't help,
being said.

The times you've kept
your secret, putting on
glasses or glancing into a page
with interest, give again
the hurt you've forgiven, pretending
to be one of us.
So the hope of love
translates as a series of hidden moments
where we like to think
someone was fooled
into it.

Who was I then
who filled these days
with illegible warnings: the marriages
broken, the land
pillaged by speculators, no word
for a stranger?

This island
where I thought the language was mine
has left me lonely
and innocent as you or that friend
who let you copy his themes
until the words became pictures
of places you would never go.

Forgive it then
that so much of after
depends on these, the words
which must find you
off the page.

Still Moment at Dun Laoghaire

for Stevie

You cross the ramp, its sure suspension
above the blue rope net
that means water not seen
for this nearness of ship to dock.
Now it is below you, a channel
you will think of as an ocean
where we met once and talked back
into a lost continent, childhood,
and a single house that keeps us sisters.

You were right to call it a language,
the way I will know that tree
blocking the view of the Peninsula
and the bluff dropping away each year
so the house must stand with conviction
flanked by the blue spruce, the swing set
waiting for our brothers' children.

Already we are more together
for how the house looks back on us.
Through the glass your face will float away
like a ship of its own
over the boundary that knows with us
the world is steady
in another view.

Look back. There is a woman
beside me, younger, older, waving
as you are waving yet,
with your blonde hair
wound and pinned, into this distance.

Woman-Enough

Figures on a silent screen,
they move into my window, its facing
on the abbey yard, six men with spades
and long-handled shovels. I had looked up
as I look up now across the strand where a small boat
has drifted into the haze of mountains
or that child walks to the end
of a dock.

Both views let in sun.
The bearded one throws off his coat
and rolls his sleeves. Two in their best clothes
from offices in London lean against a stone,
letting the shovels lift and slap.
The others dodge in and out of sun, elbow-high,
the ground thickening. The boat,
closer, one oar flashing,

pulled to the light and under, these voices
a darker blade. A wind
carries over and I hear them call out to me: 'He
was a wild one in his young days. You'll want
to lock your door.' He nods the bottle
to bring me out.

A drink to you, Peter Harte, man
that I never knew, lover
of cows and one good woman
buried across the lake.
'He was a tall man, about my size,' the one
measuring, face down in the gap.
'And wouldn't you like a big man? Big

as me?' dusting his hands on his pants and lifted out.

The boat head–on now
so it stays.

'Try it on, go down.'

The sky, the stone blue
of the sky. An edge of faces, hard looks
as though they'd hauled me live
into the open boat of their deaths, American woman,
man–enough in that country place
to stand with skulls sifted and stacked
beside the dirt pile, but woman then
where none had stood and them more men
for that mistake to see me
where he would lay.

'Not a word of this to Mary, ye hear.'

O he was a wild one,
a wild one in his youth. Sonny Peter
Harte.

On Your Own

How quickly the postures shift.
Just moments ago we seemed human
or in the Toledo of my past
I made out I was emotionally illiterate
so as not to feel a pain I deserved.

Here at the Great Southern
some of the boys have made it
into gray suits and pocket calculators.
I'm feeling end-of-season, like a somebody
who's hung around the church
between a series of double weddings.

Friend, what you said about the terror
of American Womanhood,
I forget it already, but I know
what you mean. I'm so scary some days
I'd run from myself. It's hard work
having your way, even
half the time, and having it,
know what not to do with it. Who
hasn't thrown away a life or two
at the mercy of another's passion,
spite or industry.

It's like this on your own: the charms
unlucky, the employment
solitary, the best love always
the benefit of a strenuous doubt.

Ever After

Exactly like a rain cloud
over the picnickers at the abbey
or a boat reflecting
on the peak of itself without an oar, so
my death reached everything in my mind
effortlessly.

This amazed my normal appearance
which went on swallowing
an excessive quantity of rain. An odd
expression of joy. Great sheets
of rain. Then passing

I caught the words of the mourners
like a skirt waving backwards on a scarlet road
and among them, the girl who would lay
beside me.

The long-handled shovel
from dawn to dark like a machine
and she one soft touch
for the gulls to swoop at. Cloth
buttons.

We looked at the red lights
wandering over the masts of the ships
where I was born, their dark facings in the brain,
the trees climbing side by side
with the sky into that exchange of worlds, her
hair flowing over
the river-wall. Her life, she said,

an imaginary bird let go in the white water
of January. Water that lapped

the doorstep, her short legs, her hand
on the window sill near the bridge, near
the look of the gulls
floating between the timbers.

Closing the fact of it, think
of her dead, think of a skeleton
you could embrace as the lack
of your being or lying
in this field to talk through the cry of water
into the whole future
which brings back the hands
free and ready. Think

of her. That's better. She
was at my side, the memory of her. The
wetness of the sea. I
explained to her: because you are alive
the horizon recedes. You thought you were
everything, a drum with affection, the sort
of girl to mark that page
because one hand held another
or you could skip it altogether.

If I were everything, there would be nothing
beside me. You
are beside me. The sort of girl
she was, looking out at me
through the lattices
of her hair, her
live hair.

The Sky Behind It

When it rains you remember snow.
Always there is a tree
behind it and the slant roofs thickening,
piling on sleep so the bed drifts
and you fall again into the best saving shape.

Today you noticed yourself at a distance
and the others
in the foreground, just appearances, walking
so out of harm and hope
they rose as after a dying
you saw happening to yourself alone
in a far room.

This knowing that whatever you do
it means more
than could possibly happen, that thought
and the satisfaction of music
through and around the house. If
the air could empty, you would be there
as a listening
that would move with the rooms.

To stay apart is to dream
of the house no one lives in.
You notice the snow so includes each
momentary conclusion, each
breath taking entry, that something
lasts. For once
you don't discuss it with anyone.

You go in. You
look out the window and see yourself
coming up beside the house

to knock at the window.
You let yourself in. You do
and the house shows through, dissolving
behind-the-scenes to the harmony
of a set table, space for a sigh, the vine,
the sky behind it.

So the happy ending arrives
like a membership you suspected all along.
The house is empty. You
let yourself in. You do.
You go in.

As If It Happened

She was brought up manly for a woman
to dread the tender word.
All afternoon saying goodbye
in the high ceilinged room, he
in the rocker, its fixed
reach, the whiskey troubling
their glasses.

The dull pull of the light fanned
and narrowed between them.
She had on the red handkerchief shirt.
They talked, the memory of that, two
made fearless and humble
as those who visit the dying, their live gifts
that need tending.

Say of them: 'They were lovers once'
though little stays of that.
Yet didn't the body speak? Didn't it
fly out of its heart, its faithless
goldfish of a heart? Didn't it find your house,
opened by moonlight, walking up to it,
like a masterpiece of regret: only arms, only
the bodies of so many kisses
loosed like birds against the windows, falling.

And if that night happened, if one night
I walked up to your house shared by then
with another, wouldn't you
know me? Wouldn't you
remember one night when we were holy and helpl
in each other and wouldn't you start up then
like one in terror who has dreamed himself

backwards, dreaming he could not help stepping out
at the wrong and irrevocable moment—you
stepped out.

Now they're past recalling
and that night revolves like a planet forsaken
of its days and years. Of the two
who can tell which now
is retreating, which
has stepped this way?

The Ritual of Memories

When your widow had left the graveside
and you were most alone
I went to you in that future
you can't remember yet. I brought
a basin of clear water where no tear
had fallen, water gathered like grapes
a drop at a time
from the leaves of the willow. I brought
oils, I brought a clean white gown.

'Come out,' I said, and you came up
like a man pulling himself out of a river,
a river with so many names
there was no word left for it but 'earth'.

'Now,' I said, 'I'm ready. These eyes
that have not left your face
since the day we met, wash these eyes.
Remember, it was a country road
above the sea and I was passing
from the house of a friend. Look
into these eyes where we met.'

I saw your mind go back through the years
searching for that day and finding it,
you washed my eyes
with the pure water
so that I vanished from that road
and you passed a lifetime
and I was not there.

So you washed every part of me
where any look or touch
had passed between us. 'Remember,'

I said, when you came to the feet,
'it was the night before you would ask
the girl of your village to marry. I
was the strange one. I was the one
with the gypsy look.
Remember how you stroked these feet.'

When the lips and the hands
had been treated likewise and the pit
of the throat where one thoughtless kiss
had fallen, you rubbed in the sweet oil
and I glistened like a new-made thing, not
merely human, but of the world gone past
being human.

'The hair,' I said. 'You've forgotten
the hair. Don't you know it remembers.
Don't you know it keeps everything. Listen,
there is your voice and in it the liar's charm
that caught me.'

You listened. You heard your voice
and a look of such sadness
passed over your dead face that I wanted
to touch you. Who could have known
I would be so held? Not you
in your boyish cunning; not me
in my traveler's clothes.

It's finished.
Put the gown on my shoulders.
It's no life in the shadow of another's joys.
Let me go freely now.
One life I have lived for you. This one
is mine.

The Ballad of Ballymote

We stopped at her hut
on the road to Ballymote
but she did not look up
and her head was on her knee.

What is it, we asked.
As from the dreams of the dead
her voice came up.

My father, they shot him
as he looked up from his plate
and again as he stood and again
as he fell against the stove
and like a thrush his breath
bruised the room
and was gone.

A traveler would have asked directions
but saw she would not lift her face.
What is it, he asked.

My husband sits all day in a pub
and all night and I may as well
be a widow for the way he beats me
to prove he's alive.

What is it, asked the traveler's wife,
just come up to look.

My son's lost both eyes in a fight
to keep himself a man
and there he sits behind the door
where there is no door

and he sees by the stumps
of his hands.

And have you no daughters for comfort?

Two there are and gone to nuns
and a third to the North
with a fisherman.

What are you cooking?

Cabbage and bones, she said. Cabbage
and bones.

Disappearances in the Guarded Sector

Belfast. Winter. 1976

When we stop where you lived, the house
has thickened, the entry
level to the wall with bricks, as though
it could keep you out.

Again the dream has fooled you into waking
and we have walked out
past ourselves, through the windows
to be remembered in the light
of closed rooms
as a series of impositions
across the arms of a chair, that woman's face
startled out of us so it lingers
along a brick front.

You are leading me back to the burned arcade
where you said I stood with you
in your childhood last night, your childhood
which includes me now
as surely as the look of that missing face
between the rows of houses.

We have gone so far into your past
that nothing reflects us.
No sun gleams from the glassless frame
where a room burned,
though the house stayed whole. There
is your school, your church,
the place you drank cider at lunch time.
New rows of houses are going up.
Children play quietly in a stairwell.

Walking back, you tell the story
of the sniper's bullet
making two clean holes in the taxi, how
the driver ducked and drove on
like nothing happened. No pain
passed through you; it
did not even stop the car
or make you live more
carefully. Near the check point we
stop talking, you let the hands
rub your clothes
against your body. You seem to be
there, all there.

Watching, I am more apart
for the sign of dismissal they will give me,
thinking a woman would not conceal
as I have, the perfect map
of this return where I have met
and lost you willingly
in a dead and living place.

Now when you find me next in the dream,
this boundary will move with us.
We will both come back.

Second Language

Outside, the night is glowing
with earth and rain and you
in the next room take up
your first language.
All day it has waited
like a young girl in a field.
Now she has stood up
from the straw–flattened circle
and you have taken her glance
from the hills.

The words come back.
You are with yourself again
as that child who gave up the spoon,
the bed, the horse to its colors
and uses. There is yet no hint
they would answer to anything else
and your tongue does not multiply the wrong
the stammer calling them back
and back.

You have started the one word
again, again as though it had to be made
a letter at a time
until it mends itself into saying.
The girl is beside you as lover or mother or
the aunt who visited with a kindly face
and the story of your mother
as a girl in a life before you.

She leads you across that field
to where the cows put down their wet lips
to the rust-dry trough.
But before you can get there
it will have changed. The water
will have two names
in and out of the ground. The song
you are singing, its familiar words and measures,
will be shadowed and bridged.

Remember the tune for the words.
Remember the cows for the field, those
in their sacred look who return
their great hands to the centuries of grass.

Out of sleep you are glad
for this rain, are steadied by my staying awake.
The trough will fill
and it will seem as though the dream
completes its far side.

To speak is to be robbed and clothed,
this language always mine
because so partly yours. Each word
has a crack in it to show the strain
of all it holds, all that leaks
away. Silent now, as when another
would think you sullen or
absent, you smoke after a meal, the sign
of food still on the plate, the two
chairs drawn away and angled again
into the room.

The rain enters, repeating its single word

until our bodies in their storebought clothes
make a sound against us, the dangerous visit
of the flesh perfecting its fears
and celebrations, drinking us in
by the slow unspeakable syllables.

I have forced up the screen
and put out the palm of my hand past the rush
of the eaves. In the circular glow of the porch
the lighted rain is still, is falling.

Open Fire Near a Shed

In the cab there was a song.
Not one I would have chosen, but
of which I remember, in my way,
some words without the tune. Also,
the driver, his coat. How is it
that the wrinkles in his coat-back
were almost tender? his small hands
taking from yours
my belongings.

You're stepping back now
behind the gray slats
of the gate. Your hand, the right
one, lifts through
the fine rain, causing me
to look back at myself
as your memory—a constancy
with its troubled interior
under the rained-on glass.

Looking out, I've moved already
into thought. The tunnel
on the train gives and returns my face
flickering across the winter fields,
the fields—their soft holdings
of water, of cows breathing warmly
over the tracks of birds.

Sudden then as light to the pane—
an open fire near a shed,
wilder in the stubble and light rain
for how it seems intended
to burn there
though no one is standing by.

Under Stars

The sleep of this night deepens
because I have walked coatless from the house
carrying the white envelope.
All night it will say one name
in its little tin house by the roadside.

I have raised the metal flag
so its shadow under the roadlamp
leaves an imprint on the rain-heavy bushes.
Now I will walk back
thinking of the few lights still on
in the town a mile away.

In the yellowed light of a kitchen
the millworker has finished his coffee,
his wife has laid out the white slices of bread
on the counter. Now while the bed they have left
is still warm, I will think of you, you
who are so far away
you have caused me to look up at the stars.

Tonight they have not moved
from childhood, those games played after dark.
Again I walk into the wet grass
toward the starry voices. Again, I
am the found one, intimate, returned
by all I touch on the way.

START AGAIN SOMEWHERE

'Stop, stop, you who are ragged with stars,
Die while you still have time.'

—Luis Cernuda
(tr. by John Haines)

3 A.M. Kitchen: My Father Talking

For years it was land working me, oil fields,
cotton fields, then I got some land. I
worked it. Them days you could just about
make a living. I was logging.

Then I sent to Missouri. Momma
come out. We got married.
We got some kids. Five kids.
That kept us going.

We bought some land near the water.
It was cheap then. The water
was right there. You just looked out
the window. It never left the window.

I bought a boat. Fourteen footer.
There was fish out there then.
You remember, we used to catch
six, eight fish, clean them right
out in the yard. I could of fished to China.

I quit the woods. One day just
walked out, took off my corks, said that's
it. I went to the docks.
I was driving winch. You had to watch
to see nothing fell out of the sling. If
you killed somebody you'd
never forget it. All
those years I was just working
I was on edge, every day. Just working.

You kids. I could tell you

a lot. But I won't.

It's winter. I play a lot of cards
down at the tavern. Your mother.
I have to think of excuses
to get out of the house. You're
wasting your time, she says. You're wasting
your money.

You don't have no idea, Threasie.
I run out of things
to work for. Hell, why shouldn't I
play cards? Threasie,
some days now I just don't know.

My Mother Remembers That She Was Beautiful

The falling snow has made her thoughtful
and young in the privacy
of our table with its netted candle
and thick white plates. The serious faces
of the lights breathe on the pine boards
behind her. She is visiting
the daughter never close
or far enough away to come to.

She keeps her coat on, called into
her girlhood by such forgetting
I am gone or yet
to happen. She sees herself
among the townspeople, the country glances
slow with fields and sky
as she passes or waits
with a brother in the hot animal smell
of the auction stand: sunlight,
straw hats, a dog's tail
brushing her bare leg.

'There are things you know.
I didn't have to beg,' she said, 'for anything.'

The beautiful one speaks to me
from the changed, proud face and I see
how little I've let her know
of what she becomes. Years
were never the trouble, or the white hair
I braided near the sea
on a summer day. Who

she must have been
is lost to me through some fault
in my own reflection and we will have to go on
as we think we are, walking for no one's sake
from the empty restaurant into the one color
of the snow—before us, the close houses,
the brave and wondering lights of the houses.

Harmless Streets

Many times a last time I will look
into this room like walking
fully clothed into a floodstream.
Under the candelabra in a hotel lobby or
on the train where the commuters ruffle
their papers, or standing in a corridor of
elevators, it will come before me
as though I could never leave.

When I came to you
like a woman who dressed herself in the morning,
who spread the fan of her hair
at night on your pillow, they were with us already,
those days we would live
out of what you had done alone.

You were the man of fear and omens
who cast his own death in the slant of a tree or
looking up, caused a star inside the head
to break from space, but more often
it was loss of the simplest talisman, expected,
a slight regret that could end all.

Mostly no one saw what was done. The dead
were unspectacular, scattered and inarticulate,
preferring to be handled and stepped over,
though at times they seemed to argue
among themselves, a continual racket about the beauty
of the universe or the piteousness of the human
voice, filling the ancient night
with their elaborate nostalgia.

Once there was no doubt. That one

was yours and you walked to him where he lay
and you took from his pockets
a picture, no wife or child, but an image of
himself. If he had raised up on one arm
and said in the language of the dying, 'Take this.
Remember me,' you would not have done less.
But no, the dead have no such rights and the living
are merciless, saying, 'Lie down. Be counted.'

Each day his eyes are opened on your wall
among the emblems that returned whole legions, no
survivors, but hostage to these harmless streets.
And I who did not see what was done
have seen him cut off at the neck, have heard him spe
full bodied. He is offended
there on your wall in his one death, in your one life.
He has changed his mind
and wants only to be forgotten, not entirely, no
just enough to surprise your continuing
pain. Pain that continues is not pain, outleaps

the body. That soldier
in the poster near the armchair
keeps running toward us extending his wing
of blood. It is too red. It is only the color
red. I have tried
to see it otherwise, but cannot.

You are right. What can I know, a woman
who was never there? Empathy, sad apron, I take you
on and off. In loving
it was the same. I almost
felt. Your pleasure was almost mine.

The white tree near the window

looks in on your bed, the flowered sheets
where I drift with the parachutes of the men
falling like delicate organs into watery fields.
But what can I know? I
who may not be counted, womb
of your secret shame and silences:
companion, mourner, thief.

The Meeting

for Ken Schar

My name is not my own
and you are lost in the sameness
of yours: marriage, divorce,
marriage, the name changed
like a billboard at the side of my life.

That day I saw you last
you were wearing a white suit
in the mid–winter haze.
It was too big for you.
Your shoulders didn't belong.
I heard you: 'If you feel
the rightness of a thing, do it.'

Twelve years we've come
and not a word between us.
Last night you got off a bus
in my dream. Your body
seemed too small for itself. It was
hurt by something outside my sleep.
You took off your coat.
I could see the bones of your arms.
We didn't mention it.
You asked for something ordinary
and wrong, vitamins, I think.

You had your camera on your chest
like a complicated doorknob.
You didn't open.
My hands came back
to me. I was awake in that last café
where I did not say *brother*, where
I stood apart from your sorrow

in my great young indifference.

Tired lives had run you out.
You were going away. 'Let them
have their bastard courage!'
Your hands came back
to you. You touched me, that hand
out of the grave. Early
and late, this hour has closed
around us.

Start Again Somewhere

Don't let her stop you this time, Miguel,
though this isn't your name
and you won't look back
if she calls to you.
For today you are Miguel Ricardo
of the daggers and stallions. Already
you are galloping away
on the great sexual beast
of your refusals.

No, Miguel, it isn't right.
No man who loves truly
should stand for it. And anyway, she
couldn't have cared much, the way she got
prettier and prettier for her own sweet
sake, tossing her hair
from the high arched brows,
looking away.

We've seen her type—the soft mouth
and the set of the head like a dare.
Who could resist?
You only did well to catch yourself
in time. Before your heart
made a mess of it. Before
you did something you could live
to regret.

But we were watching you,
those of us who know better
than to take such chances.
You didn't go too far
and now you've set yourself straight.

And you did it just right, Miguel, taking all
the blame like that so she couldn't
hate you, so she'd have to
think of you the rest of her life
as someone she should have loved better.

You're not young, Miguel, but there's time,
time to find that woman
you adored in your youth, the one
who married the butcher and stayed
in the same town raising his sons, scraping
the maps of blood from his aprons.

All in all we're proud of you.
We see you're no fool.
You wouldn't give something for
nothing. To be a fool
takes devotion of the most pigheaded sort.
You have to want one thing in the wrong place
so badly you make it a way of life.
You forget what it costs.
You forget that others see what it
costs you. And at night

when the butcher's wife
takes her red hands from the water
you are there to kiss them, though you close
your eyes, though secretly
you have galloped away
like the fool you are, but a fool
of your own choosing, wasting
the soft lips of her over
and over in the starved corners.

Backdrop With Lovers, 1931

She's wearing a cotton dress
and sits on his lap casually, her arm
swung around his neck, as though she knew
this would happen, that moment, his hand
on her breast. Now we're all caught out here
in eternity by their expression in the singular.
Things were franker then?
Then. What may not be,
stopped.

Just as a quiver overtakes the landscape,
so each friendly beginning
is a hazard of sweet faces, birds flushed suddenly
from the lilac. Or because your manner
years later chooses an utter hopefulness,
we're made unequal
as the crowd parted by a blind walker. We
step aside and the calm planet of his head glides by.
That moment our thoughts stare
back at us, the nearest face closed
deeply into space.

She, then seventeen, could listen
while singing—her small wrists. Softly,
the important act takes place
without us, and she is crone now
or dead where painted treetops edge the blur
reminding. All that—years, backyards, sunning
in a neck-tie halter on the cellar door, whole cemete
of hopefulness have broken from sight
before the shutter. 'Hold still, hold it!' one voice

still trying to check our disappearance
between the makeshift stars. Behind them, the waves,
stylized, restless as party hats. Just looking
we are flying with multitudes
into their future, the open boat and backdrop
skimming into floodlights in the pines, where, where?
Your knowing, not to ask.

Counterfeit Kisses

You want me to think these
are the real thing. I
can do that, take them one
after the other for all
they're worth. I'll close
my eyes in the usual way, put my
hand around the back
of your neck. Yes, I'm drinking in
these little death's head profiles;
they're getting by
with their sloppy noses, their slack
jaws, their approximate double
chins. Just think of them
milling around down there
in the underworld of used up
affection, strutting about
with their little heart-shaped
mirrors, tweaking each other's false
moustaches, comparing
the authenticating sixth wrinkle
in a brow. Who wouldn't trade
a kingdom of exact replicas
for one city of such believable fakes?
To you, dear bandit of my free
exchange, I give full value, lip
for shining lip, without the love
of difference. I can spare you
every one.

Hybrid

It will be gradual, this imposition
of the grotesque. No matter,
the candles burn the same in the entry.
Apples still drop with the rain
in the orchard as by a sudden
irreversible stroke.

'Little–turnip–blood' the gardeners
have called you, after their
affection for failures. Regardless,
you are sure you've seen your kind before.
That propensity for backing into turnstiles,
those embroidered hankies
found on your person, linking you
to a mother.

On display next to the mule
you realize it could end here. The lights
of the fireflies perplex
their trial mating with the moth: off–
on–off. You look
to the mule, but
his eyes have gone under.

To be singular but hearty
makes him self–intimate. He does not see you
becoming someone you
will never meet, the one who approaches now
with that over–familiar look, insisting
you are of at least
two minds.

The Same Kiss After Many Years

Like a cat haunting the familiar porch,
it's found us again, we
who meet now only to hear
what didn't happen to us, but to them,
those two we sent away
into lives we wanted
to see happening to us.

They've done well for themselves, as
expected. He's an artist. His work
sells. She's aged, but well,
from her bones out, has
travel plans, time yet
to pick and choose.

We're fond of them, not
just parental. Who else would listen
to us as we were
and take the blame
with such sad-eyed equanimity? They
know better now, would do it
over if they could.

We love their fateful hesitations,
self-caresses, the glance
that tells us plainly
there are those who await
their reappearance elsewhere. We're
concerned not to have them
missed, so this will happen
painlessly, leaving us all
the better for it.

They'll go back refreshed, seeing
how little we amounted to. Good
they got out when they did.
Let them kiss now, in the old
impassioned way, and go about their
business. They do it well, that
independence with a touch
of remorse. You're right. They're
better than we ever were. Kiss me.
Let's forget them.

If Never Again

for Art Homer

Taken singly, these depend on you
to be lucky without paying anyone back.
No admiration or accident we like your name.
It reminds us of baseball and poets
with batting averages who could
swing it. I saw you dancing once
with your hair on. It was fine, such
intelligent hair, so live it could do without
you and still be faithful as any covering we hope
to last. Otherwise, we'd call you 'Legs'

for all those perilous childhood trips
to the store, spending the change on popsicles
the mean kids angled to knock
in the dirt. You learned to lick fast and run
'like hell', taking the icy lumps into you.
I was a mean kid once myself, but
recovered. We had to watch ourselves, even us,
for worse ones. No one was safe, not dogs,
not Jo-Jo taking his glass eye out
to trade his way home past the gulley. If

you deserved abuse we would give you a flashlight
and send you on a long apology
to the neighborhood. That would be plenty—
appeasing the lifetime of a fence or stones
painted white to border pansies. There goes your
little light, bobbing the houses up
from the dark. Over your shoulder, 'rolling in',
there's fog. You never felt closer. You
could even be you, despite their theories of
former lives and momentary personalities.
Aren't you that kid who ran errands for grandma?
so shy, so sweet. Getting lost near home

wasn't even worthwhile. They'd just find you
something foreign to do like taking out
the garbage. It got your hands
mixed up with the atmosphere
the way a pair of wings flew into the house once
and gave the mirrors something ambitious
to think about. There was a patch
of couch coming into the frame near the mantle
when the bird struck. It
got through our eyes to the windows, then
dodged into itself again as feathers. So
mirrors say we're enough to go around
or come back the same if we look
away. Such dreary lessons could make you
wrong. The bird still thinks the room
will give in to sky. Do you know better?
Holding the door and calling 'out, out'
as though it were obvious. Only the bird is
open, veering with curtains and all that loose
breakage of memorables. You were flying years
when you noticed that house over you. Courage
they called it, so you belonged, taking it all
with you, the house, its habitual nestings
and preenings, that mother in her backward
longing, lifting you again and again
from the small, mossy bed.

Your Letter Is Being Written Without Y

Some dreams let you keep happening
with your eyes open. Others
and you're cut off
like a door scrambling for its house.
I can't do anything for you. Which is
not to say I wouldn't.
We have to swing here. Every now
and then, our feet brush
or that tree, that bird bends down.
We'll have to laugh to make it out of here,
or fall into seriousness, the way snow
falls into your hat, not mentioning,
but making a little headway
into a little dark
the size of where a head would go.

We were hovering near the gate
and one of us wasn't going home. One
of those moments to make a promise or walk away
with your collar up. I wanted to spoil, eat
Mexican food with lots of hot stuff
to get my edge up. But you were back
in your childhood, lying still
under the roses, pretending to be dead
for the neighbor kid. She had heart murmur
and her mother told you, 'don't
let her run.' When you think like that
she runs to you
and no matter how you want to, your legs
won't, and the distance shortens her
into a little heartbeat with hands and a mother.

You still walk around covered with roses
for her sake. And who was she? Only
leading into later? into where we stand, above
and beyond the gate like bad handwriting
across a night sky with smoke, with
a little more to say
before the sky runs out or the dark
fades and we are daylight. Outside its dream,
the head stands with its eyes wide open,
and putting the hat on, its head
of snow, we are going
to take each other by the wing, by the way

we would want to be remembered
in someone else's childhood, as serious as that,
under the roses, to keep them
breathing, I would do that
for you, if I could, showing off
to break out what I mean, what I mean to be
to you—if need be—can. This written
as we are, over the envelope, to be read by tearing
the words up, their little diplomas.

Mr. Sad–to–say, we are very much
and alive. To you,
what I can, without you.